To all Zambians -

Hoping that digitalization will foster prosperity in the country

July 2023

IMPRINT

© 2023 Karin Moder (Editor)

Graphic design of book cover:
Danny Chiyesu (Digital Majik) and Morgan Mulenga (Radicity Brands)
Zambia Map (p. 6): based on wikipedia.de + additions by Radicity
Brands Publisher: BATCH Solutions, Zambia
Distributor: African Books Collective, UK
ISBN: 978-9982-43-438-6

Digital Zambia

Mobile Money & More

Karin Moder (Editor)

Lusaka - Frankfurt am Main

LIST OF ABBREVIATIONS

DQL	Digital Quality of Life
GDP	Gross Domestic Product
ICT	Information and Communication Technology
IDES	Inclusive Digital Economy Scorecard
LDC	Least Developed Country
MNO	Mobile Network Operator
SIM	Subscriber Identification Module
SMEs	Small and Medium Enterprises
TEVETA	Technical Education, Vocational and Entrepreneurship Training Authority
UNCDF	United Nations Capital Development Fund
ZICTA	Zambia Information and Communications Technology Authority
ZRA	Zambia Revenue Authority

TABLE OF CONTENTS

INTRODUCTION 8

DIGITALIZATION: ZAMBIA'S OVERALL STATUS 10
THE INCLUSIVE DIGITAL ECONOMY SCORECARD (IDES) 13

E-FINANCE: MOBILE MONEY & MORE 18
THE EVOLUTION OF PLAYERS IN THE MOBILE MONEY MARKET 19
WHY DO ZAMBIANS USE MOBILE MONEY? 20
GROWTH FACTORS 25
STRUCTURE AND ASSESSMENT OF MOBILE MONEY PROVIDERS 30
STARTUPS AND INNOVATION... 33

E-COMMERCE: SHOPPING ONLINE IN BIG CITIES 36
ONLINE SURVEY RESULTS 37
Interview with Afshon Wallace Ngige (AWN)................................... 42

E-EDUCATION: EARLY STEPS AND LATER CHALLENGES 46
VOCATIONAL TRAINING 49
Interview with Dr. Phillip Mwansa... 52

E-GOVERNMENT: COMPREHENSIVE E-TAX SYSTEMS 56
Interview with Chinedu Koggu (CK).. 60
Interview with Misheck Kakonde (MK)... 67

OUTLOOK 71

ANNEX: 73
1. WRITERS' PROFILES 73
2. WITH GRATITUDE AND JOY 74
3. DQL Index sub-criteria list 76
4. REFERENCES 77

"We are in the digital age now".
(Danny Chiyesu, Zambian visual artist, 2017)

INTRODUCTION

"Digital Zambia" tells a story about digitalization in Zambia – a land-locked country, rich in natural resources, with 19-20 million inhabitants in Southern Africa. But is this a relevant topic in a country which - like most countries in Southern African - still faces "serious" challenges to adequately feed its citizens according to the Global Hunger Index (GHI)[1]? And is it a story worth telling and sufficiently rich in a world where AI-based innovations like ChatGPT can win one million registrations in just five days and standards of technological sophistication are seemingly shifted in the blink of an eye?

Our answer is yes. Yes it is worthwhile exploring "Digital Zambia", even if by common standards digitalization is more advanced on other continents and even if some other African countries fare better in rankings of digital transformation. Zambians are generally tech-savvy as one of our interview partners stated, but they have to come up with a number of challenges that are not common in the so-called developed world, e.g. the major power-cuts lasting between 4 and 12 hours per day, which Zambia had to face from late January to end of February 2023. Such impediments are likely to slow down the process of digital transformation, but access to new technologies such as satellite-based internet services might counterbalance some of the challenges, especially the marked deficits in broadband connectivity for users in remote areas of Zambia. In June 2023,

---
[1] Welthungerhilfe, CONCERN worldwide (2022), p.15-16

satellite connectivity provider Starlink has been awarded an operating license by the Zambian Government, following tests across nine Zambian provinces.

Zambia's ranking in the Digital Quality of Life Index (DQL), which we will feature in the first chapter, has decreased from 2021 to 2022, but so has China's. We will look at the bigger picture through the DQL lens as well as the Inclusive Digital Economy Scorecard (IDES) and hear about relative strengths as well as shortcomings. After that we will shed light on digitization in selected areas such as e-finance, e-commerce, e-education and e-government. On this journey we will happily showcase Mobile Money as part of the e-finance landscape, since it is considered a major success story in Zambia's digital transformation and a noteworthy contributor to economic development through financial inclusion. The information provided in this e-book comes in different shapes, including figures, graphs, historic reviews, survey results and full-length interviews besides a number of screenshots from relevant websites and internet portals. Thus, we will provide interesting and engaging insights into "Digital Zambia" – both to Zambian and non-Zambian readers.

Karin Moder

DIGITALIZATION: ZAMBIA'S OVERALL STATUS
(by Karin Moder)

Digitalization is high up on political agendas all over the world. In September 2021, in his maiden speech to the National Assembly, Zambian President Hakainde Hichilema underlined the importance of digital transformation for human, social, political and economic activities and pointed out to the creation of the new Ministry of Technology and Science. It is thus interesting to look at the bigger picture first, and get some insights about the state of digital transformation in Zambia. What are relevant indicators, which describe where Zambia stands and will most likely head to?

Let's start with the "Digital Quality of Life (DQL) Index", which was developed by cyber security company Surfshark and first published in 2019. The DQL ranking analyses the overall digital quality of life according to five main indicators, which are internet affordability, internet quality, e-infrastructure, e-security and e-government. These main indicators aggregate 14 inter-related sub-indicators[2].

In 2021, Zambia was - for the first time - included in the DQL index and ranked 94th out of 110 countries, with a ranking index of 0.38 (https://surfshark.com). Thus, Zambia was not in a leading DQL position, but still had some rankings which stood out: Mobile affordability was an indicator which placed Zambia above 102 other countries (rank no.8). Besides, the speed of broadband growth was higher than in almost 100 other countries (#13). And mobile speed growth turned out to be an indicator which made Zambia rank just slightly below average (#48).

---

[2] The 14 sub-indicators are presented on p.76 in the annex.

Screenshot 1: Selected Zambia DQL Rankings (2021)

Source: https://surfshark.com/dql2021?country=ZM

Meanwhile the results of the 2022 DQL index ranking have been uploaded. Zambia has lost some ground and ranks 105th out of 117 countries – a drop by 11 ranks. The weaker performance in the DQL index goes hand in hand with a lesser ranking in the sub-indicator Mobile Affordability (#81). Also, Broadband Speed Growth and Mobile Speed Growth have comparatively decreased (#107 and #70). Interestingly, the sub-indicator where Zambia ranks best out of all 14 sub-indicators is cyber security (#51). This seems to imply that cyber security issues are better taken care of in Zambia or pose less of a problem compared to more than 50 other countries.

Overall, Zambia ranks 15 out of the 23 African countries listed in the 2022 DQL index. The country reaches a slightly higher score than most of its geographic neighbours in Eastern and Southern Africa, especially the Democratic Republic of Congo (#117), but clearly falls behind Kenya (#78) and South Africa (#66), the DQL no. 1 in Africa.

Screenshot 2: 2022 DQL Rankings for 4 Selected African Countries

Source: https://surfshark.com/dql2022/dql-compare?table=true&country1=ZM&country2=KE&country3=ZA&country4=CD

The following screenshot shows a map of African countries' 2022 DQL rankings and provides a helpful visual overview. The countries coloured in grey – mostly in West or Central Africa – have not (yet) been integrated into the DQL index ranking.

Screenshot 3: DQL Africa Ranking (2022)

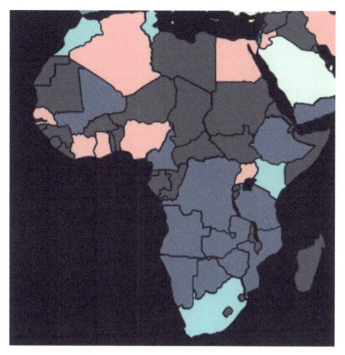

Source: https://surfshark.com/dql2022/statistics

THE INCLUSIVE DIGITAL ECONOMY SCORECARD (IDES)

The other tool worth viewing in detail is the "Inclusive Digital Economy Scorecard" (IDES), which was developed by the United Nations Capital Development Fund (UNCDF)[3]. Here, some of the

---

[3] The refining of IDES was supported by a reference group of several organizations (GSMA, EU, UNDP, UNCTAD, UN-DESA and ADB) and governments of four least developed countries (LDCs):

indicators used in the DQL index reappear. However, its scope is bigger and also encompasses factors, which would not be relevant for individual users or companies.

> *"The Inclusive Digital Economy Scorecard is a strategic performance and policy tool that has been developed to support countries set the priorities for their country's digital transformation. It identifies the key market constraints hindering the development of an inclusive digital economy and helps set the right priorities with public and private stakeholders ..." (https://ides.uncdf.org/about/scorecard)*

All IDES indicators fall into four main categories, which describe some kind of wholistic ecosystem of digital transformation and are illustrated below:

Figure 1: Set of Relevant IDES Indicators

Policy & Regulation	Infrastructure
<ul><li>Active Government Promotion</li><li>Active Policy Promotion</li><li>Digital Economy Regulation</li></ul>	<ul><li>ID Infrastructure</li><li>Connectivity</li><li>ICT Usage and Ownership</li><li>Digital Payment</li></ul>

Burkina Faso, Nepal, Solomon Islands and Uganda. According to the UNCDF website the reference group also had a share in driving the measurement of inclusive digital economies.

Innovation	Skills
• Community Development • Level of Skills • Supporting Infrastructure • Investment	• Basic Skills • Digital Literacy • Financial Literacy

Source: https://ides.uncdf.org/about/scorecard

The Zambian IDES score was gathered in 2021, from a situational analysis with diverse stakeholders, which also included SWOT analysis. The results were published by the Ministry of Technology and Science, partnering with UNCDF.

The overall IDES score attributed to Zambia amounts to 45%, which places the country at the top end of the so-called start-up phase for digital transformation – close to the next phase of expansion (ranging up to 75%)[4]. The following map shows some Central and Southern African countries and their assessment in the IDES system. Like Zambia (see embryo shape), her direct neighbours Tanzania and the Democratic Republic of Congo are placed in the start-up segment of digital transformation, whereas Uganda is coloured in darker blue to mark the expansion stage.

---

[4] The Digital Inclusiveness Score amounts to 53%. As a consequence, the digital divide is placed at 47%.

Screenshot 4: Map of African Countries with IDES Scores (2021)[5]

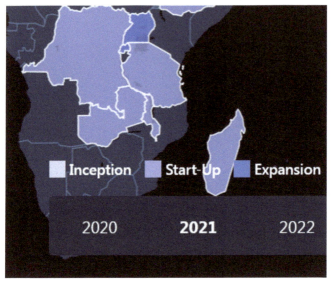

Source: https://ides.uncdf.org/

As the following diagram shows, Zambia's IDES score benefits most from achievements in the policy and regulation section, whereas the innovation segment has the largest negative effect on the overall score. Infrastructure and Skills are placed in between.

---

[5] As of July 29, 2023, updated IDES Scores for 2022 were not yet available.

Figure 2: Zambia's IDES Scores

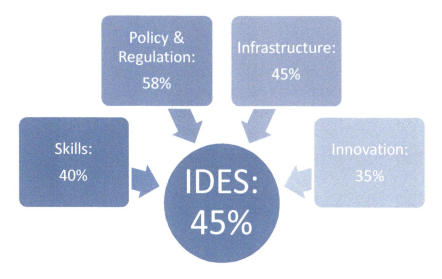

Source: Author's own construction

Following the deduction of the IDES score, Zambia's Minister of Technology and Science Felix C. Mutati summarized the major bottlenecks to increased adoption of digital technologies as follows[6]:

- Low smartphone penetration
- Limited last mile connectivity
- Poor digital skills, and
- Inadequate platforms to deliver digital services as well as limited support for digital innovation and entrepreneurship.

These issues will be illustrated in more detail in the following chapters which provide sectoral analysis and will shed some light on achievements and impediments in the respective sectors.

---

[6] Republic of Zambia / UNCDF (2022), p. 4

E-FINANCE: MOBILE MONEY & MORE
(by Edna Kabala Litana, Karin Moder and Lombe M. Chibesakunda)

The evolution of money has seen many transitions - from material goods and services to shells and beads, gold and paper money, until it reached an added layer of abstraction, namely the digital existence and transfer of money. Zambia was among the first countries to adopt electronic financial services (e-finance) in Africa. Over the last decade, there has been significant growth in digital financial services and mobile money in Zambia. In particular mobile money payments have grown by 130% in value from 2021 to 2022. Several causal factors have facilitated this growth trajectory.

Since the emergence of the first service to bank the unbanked in Kenya, mobile money, a form of digital money, has gained wide acceptance in developing countries such as Zambia. Mobile money typically refers to a financial transaction made by using a Subscriber Identification Module (SIM)-enabled device such as a cellular phone via a mobile network (Donovan, 2012).

Typically, money is deposited into the account by physically giving cash to an agent, in return for electronic money. Mobile money can thus be considered as the provision of a range of financial services, including transfer of money, via a mobile phone and mobile network operator. Individuals are free to make withdrawals of the money from mobile money accounts. In order to withdraw money, electronic money is transferred via the mobile phone to the agent's electronic money account and cash is received in return. However, depositors do not receive interest on their electronic accounts and bear the risk of loss of value through inflation (Aron & Muellbauer, 2019[7]).

THE EVOLUTION OF PLAYERS IN THE MOBILE MONEY MARKET

As an early adopter of mobile money services around 2009, Zambia has witnessed various players on the mobile money landscape. Zoona launched the very first mobile money service in Zambia and was initially renowned for offering value-added services beyond mobile wallets. Particularly, Zoona offered creative and unique bulk payments, business-to-business payments and e-voucher services to donors, governments and private corporations. For instance, settlement of payments for cotton farmers was made through Zoona. Later, mobile network operators (MNOs) Airtel and MTN also introduced services in 2011 and 2012 respectively.

Airtel and MTN were set apart from Zoona since they provided users with money transfer, bill payment, savings and credit access services. Their services were also deemed relatively affordable compared to Zoona and thus tailored to driving inclusive finance. In particular, they took advantage of the main ideas around consumer goods that are low priced in nature and targeted the mass market as the main payment platform (Ngambi, 2016).

As Airtel and MTN gained tremendous popularity across mobile money users, Zoona changed its business model to have more focus entirely on growing its money transfer service to clients in rural and urban areas. With the growth in the number of mobile phone users also encouraging growth in mobile money usage on the Airtel and

---

[7] Aron, J. and Muellbauer, 2019. The Economics of Mobile Money: Harnessing the Transformative Power of Technology to Benefit the Global Poor. Available: https://voxeu.org/article/economics-mobile-money.

MTN platforms, Zoona, however, faced fierce competition and was pushed out of business between 2016 and 2018 (Informant #1, interview on June 21, 2021).

A third mobile money operating licence was granted to the Zambia Telecommunications Company (Zamtel) in 2014. After 3 years of system in-house testing, Zamtel finally launched the Zamtel Kwacha in 2017, branding itself as a government operator with a very affordable platform fee structure relative to its competitors.

WHY DO ZAMBIANS USE MOBILE MONEY?

Mobile money is a popular technology among Zambians. It helps overcome problems from weak institutional infrastructure and the cost structure of conventional banking. For instance, for the poor people in Zambia, mobile money accounts are mostly affordable and do not require the minimum balance requirements and regular charges like typical bank accounts. In fact, mobile phone technology has the advantage that consumers themselves invest in a mobile phone handset, while the (scalable) infrastructure is already in place for the widespread distribution of airtime through secure network channels. An exemplary user, informant (R1)[8], noted:

---

[8] Interview with (R1) held on 12th November, 2021, with (R2) on 9th November, 2021.

"I don't have a job and regular income ... This discourages me to open a formal bank account which would require more money. But since I have a small handset, I can also bank using mobile money. When I sell my cassava to ensure I have some money to buy food for my children, I save whatever remains in my mobile money account. It's cheaper to save using mobile money because there are many booths around and one can even save a K5 per day. For banks, it's hard, we hear that one must have a book balance of about K500 before they can use their bank account. ... With mobile money, the fact that I can save the little I have from my cassava business and get charged as little as K2.5 for a withdraw of so much money like K100, it makes mobile money more useful. Mobile money is cheap and convenient for me to even use for increasing my savings and one day, to expand my business..."

Mobile money is not only popular for being a facility for private storage of funds among Zambians. It has also been renowned for being a safe way to transfer money and make payments for bills. Some users claim that the actual cost of transactions such as payment for electricity, cable television and water bills is reduced because one can easily make such transactions instantly using their phone. Users also hold the view that transaction costs associated with sending and receiving money are significantly reduced with mobile money, as informant (R2) shared:

"I have been using Airtel Money to buy electricity units and pay for my Nkana water bill. It's cheaper for me because I don't have to get on a bus from here in Kwacha to town to pay the bills through ZESCO and Nkana Water and Sewerage offices. ... Now, with Airtel money, I just pay over the phone and I get charged about K1 for each bill payment... Now, it's much easier for me to send money to those that urgently need it. For example, during the farming season, I just send money to my father using my mobile money account and he instantly receives it. I just add what I'd have used for transport and it goes a long way in terms of buying farming inputs for my father in the village. For him to withdraw the money, he is just charged a small amount of money... Mobile money reduced these costs of paying bills and sending money in my case..."

The popularity of mobile money has also extended to its use in networks of women's savings groups. Recently, in most communities of Zambia, women's savings groups instill a sense of belonging and are important for the subsistence of lives. In the event of hardships, women turn to these groups to smooth out consumption and meet the daily expenses of life. Different communities in Zambia have organized groups that are individually regulated with little to no intervention by the state. Women typically come together to ensure that they save money as a group using mobile money. Their groups normally comprise of about 10-20 people and the women agree on a weekly or monthly amount of money that each individual contributes. They also agree to lend the pooled amounts of savings to each other at a reasonable interest rate. At the end of a savings cycle, the women share the total amount of money saved and do so by transferring each member's share to their mobile money account. A Kitwe business woman (R3)[9] explained:

> "...I belong to a savings group with 20 women from my former school. We agree to save a minimum of K300 each per month and we have 3 treasurers or admins. We all use digital interaction and have virtual meetings about our savings group using WhatsApp. We transact using Airtel or MTN mobile money. We send our monetary obligations to our treasurers' mobile money accounts at an agreed date. If one delays, they are charged a penalty and this is in very rare cases because we all know each other and encourage each other to be diligent in our payments. We also agree to borrow from the pooled savings at an interest rate of 10%. The accumulated interest at the end of the year is shared across the members and in addition to this, all members go away with their savings. I always borrow to boost investment in my business of selling second hand bed sheets. Other women borrow to buy property such as land, pay rentals or pay school fees for their children. Sometimes, life can get expensive and hard, and in such cases, members borrow from the group to buy food and pay for other basic necessities. ... We have so far successfully run 2 cycles and each cycle is 12 months. This would have not been possible without mobile money because it's easy, reliable, instant and transparent. ... All we agree to do is if one can't use their mobile phone to send money, they go to a mobile money booth in town or in the community and send the money..."

---

[9] Interview held on 12th November, 2021.

Mobile money also made the highest contribution to the country's financial inclusion statistics compared to other competing channels of financial inclusion (Figure 1). Spreading financial services through mobile money to the financially underserved areas in the country has been comparatively easy with communications technology; mobile money only requires the use of mobile phones and so far, the country has over 90 percent of the population with mobile phone access (ZICTA, 2020[10]).

Table 1: Financial Sector Players and Contribution to Financial Inclusion (%)

	2015	2020
Capital Markets	0.3	0.3
Microfinance	1.3	2.1
Insurance	2.8	5.0
Pensions	3.8	8.2
Banks	24.8	20.7
Mobile money	14.0	58.5

Source: Finscope study (2020)

It is worth-while noting that users of mobile money benefit from reduced pecuniary and non-pecuniary costs. The latter are overheads associated with coordination costs between individuals and costs of delays in transactions and long waiting times in queues during money transfer or bill settlement transactions.

---

[10] Zambia Information and Communications Technology Authority (ZICTA), 2020. ICT Statistics Portal and Database. https://www.zicta.zm/

GROWTH FACTORS

Mobile money has undoubtedly experienced positive growth and acceptance among Zambians. Figure 3 illustrates that the growth in volumes of mobile money transactions was on a steady increase between 2012 and 2017, but recorded more rapid increases between 2017 and 2020. This could indicate that more people paid bills, transferred money across social networks, saved or invested using mobile money.

Figure 3: Trends in Mobile Money growth in Zambia (volumes)

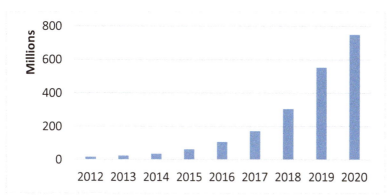

Source: ZICTA 2020

Coincidentally, the period in which mobile money started to grow rapidly, was associated with the negative effects of the COVID-19 pandemic and characterized by less physical interaction during transactions. In late 2020 and early 2021, with rising infection rates, trading and social spaces only opened for a few hours and in extreme cases closed to the public, e.g. restaurants and bars. Amidst social distancing calls, campaigns for people to stay home and embrace the use of digital platforms as a substitute for in-contact transactions, mobile money became a highly encouraged way to pay bills, make remittances and generally transact. According to the Bank of Zambia, volumes of mobile payments increased by 35.8% to 750 million in 2020[11]. Mobile money has since become a more renowned channel for settlement of payments during difficult times, as informant (R4)[12] elucidates:

> "In August, 2021, my elder brother in Northern Province had Covid. During the time he was sick, I could call the doctor who would give me some ideas of medicines to buy for him. I would just send money to my brother's wife in Northern Province using Airtel money and MTN Money and she would buy medicine for him. Mobile money allowed me to pay for my brother's medication miles away. During times like these where Covid limits physical interaction and people are discouraged from taking money or medicines to loved ones in need, mobile money offers a practical solution…".

Besides growth in annual volumes of MoMo, it is very interesting to view growth in value of mobile money payments, which has been especially pronounced since 2019.

---

[11] https://www.boz.zm/June_2021.pdf
[12] Interview held on 10th November, 2021.

Figure 4:   Mobile Money Value of Payments (2013 – 2022)

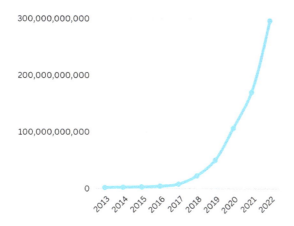

Source: Bank of Zambia, 2023, Monthly Payments Report
https://www.boz.zm/payment-systems-statistics.htm

Over a period of just five years the value of mobile money transactions increased from K7.29 billion in 2017 to K295.83 billion in 2022. As of 2022, there are more than 11 million active subscribers of mobile money wallets, with a jump in growth of more than 100% in 2020 due to Covid-19.

Table 2: Trends in Volumes and Values of Mobile Money Transactions

	2020	2021	2022
Volumes of Transactions	746,500,187	843,121,817	843,068,499
Values of Transactions (ZMW)	105,619,623,780	169,402,432,643	295,828,075,728
Active Subscribers	8,607,461	9,867,409	11,246,686

Source: Bank of Zambia

SURPASSING NUMBER OF BANK ACCOUNTS

In 2017, mobile money accounts in the Zambia reached close to 4 million, surpassing the current existing number of bank accounts by 1 million (Malakata, 2017).

Several causal factors have facilitated the significant growth in the mobile money sector. Besides technological infrastructure developments, both the creation of a regulatory framework on e-money/ mobile money and interoperability of payments systems have been key factors. Safeguarding the interests of consumers by ensuring that mobile money services are safe and secure has also contributed to an increase in the number of users.

In Zambia, government regulation for digital payments across the country was launched as early as in 2007 through the Payment Systems Act. Under this umbrella the Bank of Zambia (BoZ) implemented directives to provide incentives for accelerated digital payments. Interbank settlements started in 2014 with the Zambia Electronic Clearing House (ZECHL), a non-profit organization equally held by BoZ and BoZ member banks, acting as a facilitator of the respective settlements. There have also been other significant factors and regulatory innovations which have contributed to the MoMo success story in Zambia, e.g. the Electronic Payments Directives enabling fintech companies to start operations and electronic money business as well as the National Financial Switch (NFS). The NFS allows financial institutions across Zambia to exchange digital payments by linking clearing systems - where the bank verifies user funds - and fund transfer systems. The switch officially went live in 2018, but only enabled clearing at point of sale (POS) in 2019 and switching at ATMs in 2020.

Adding to this, in 2022, Bank of Zambia Governor Denny Kalyaya launched the ' Go Cashless' campaign, through which citizens have been encouraged to use more digital payment methods.

As already indicated, the number of active MoMo subscribers depends on a variety of causal factors. In international benchmarking, internet connectivity is usually seen as one of the key factors. The following comparison may, however, illustrate the role, which other factors play. When comparing value of MoMo transaction numbers in Zambia and Malawi, one can see that in Malawi the share of people using the internet is twice as high as in Zambia. The value of transactions in Zambia, however, is double the value of Malawi.

This leaves considerable room for other factors which determine the value of mobile money transactions such as the population size of the country and its state of development. In this regard Kenya can be seen as the African champion - an African country, with a tech-savvy population of about 53 million people, which can pride itself in both high internet penetration and high total value of MoMo transactions.

Table 3: Value of MoMo Transactions and Internet Usage in Selected African Countries

Country	Total Value of Transactions 2020	Total Value of Transactions 2021	Total Value of Transactions 2022	Rank	Internet Usage
Zambia	$5 billion	$10 billion	$15 billion	7	28%
Malawi	$800 million	$4.7 billion	$6.7 billion	15	56%
Kenya	$40 billion	$53 billion	$61 billion	4	81%

Source: Bank of Malawi, 2023, Monthly Payments Report; Bank of Zambia, 2023, Monthly Payments Report; Bank of Kenya, 2023, Monthly Payments Report

STRUCTURE AND ASSESSMENT OF MOBILE MONEY PROVIDERS

The current mobile money provider ecosystem centers around high volume companies, which are mainly MNOs (MTN, Airtel, Zamtel). Both MTN and Airtel's mobile money businesses share an identical fee structure, which involves charges of K2.50 for withdrawals of K1 – K150[13]. The scheme ends with the highest tier of K100 for transactions of K5,000 – K10,000.

Official information about the MNO's respective market share and numbers of monthly users is scarce. At the end of 2020, ITWeb quoted Airtel with a monthly user base of 3 million and MTN with 4.5 million users. It seems that no official updates have since been made available by the MNOs and respective letters and e-mails of inquiry to MTN and Airtel officials on April 6, 2023, have not received a

---

[13] https://www.airtel.co.zm/assets/pdf/AIRTEL-Tariff-Guide-Poster-A1.pdf
https://www.mtn.zm/how-to/momo-tariffs/

response by the time of concluding this book. We will thus consider mobile telephone subscription market share figures as an approximation of the 2022 market shares in the mobile money business.

Figure 5: MNO's Mobile Telephone Subscription Market Shares (2022)

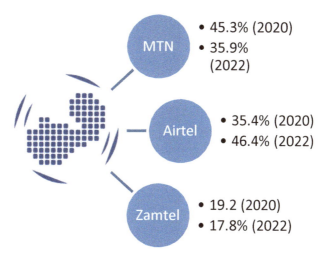

- 45.3% (2020)
- 35.9% (2022)

- 35.4% (2020)
- 46.4% (2022)

- 19.2 (2020)
- 17.8% (2022)

Source: ZICTA (2022). Annual Market Report

As can be seen, MTN Zambia has lost market leadership to Airtel Zambia in the course of two years. It is thus highly likely that Airtel's mobile money user base has also significantly increased since 2020 and has reached a value clearly beyond 3 million users. At the same time, we also expect that MTN has registered a certain increase in monthly users of mobile money within the same two-year period.

MTN Group is the largest fintech group in Africa, with its mobile money arm valued at $5 billion in 2021. According to Bloomberg, Airtel Africa's mobile money business was valued at $2.65 billion in 2021. Both Zambian MNOs are reported to operate their mobile money businesses at a respective loss.

Customer sentiment is mixed about the two mobile money providers. In a social media sentiment analysis[14] most MTN users appeared to believe that their mobile money services had been poor in terms of the customer complaint system, fraudulent activities and reversal transactions while others felt that their services have been favourable as to ease of processes on the platform.

Comments about Airtel Mobile Money weighed more on the negative side as well and centered around glitches in the system, inability to do reservals and the system being slow. The few positive results focused on accessibility and the ease in which Airtel Mobile Money can be used. According to the researchers, the predominance of negative comments may be because dissatisfaction is expressed more often than satisfaction.

It's also worth noting that there might be regional preferences by subscribers, so that in certain urban areas certain preferences for one mobile money operator over another can be identified. MTN seems to be the preferred operator on the Copperbelt, whereas Airtel appears to be the favoured provider in Lusaka.

---

[14] The sentiment analysis was first conducted by ProBase Group in June 2022 . The team collected more than 100 unique comments/feedback on each mobile operator, including comments on the app store, twitter, Facebook and Reddit. The team verified the information and that users were from the Zambian market. Each comment was then ranked in the following order: Very negative, negative, neutral, positive, very positive.

STARTUPS AND INNOVATION

Besides the big players, recent years have seen some start-ups staging innovations in the field of digital finance. There is a selection of companies such as Spenn, Kazang and Yellow Card which have built strong markets based on payment wallet solutions.

Figure 6: Startups in Digital Finance

\multicolumn{2}{c	}{Start-ups}
SPENN	**KAZANG**
- offers a blockchain based mobile wallet to users, - gained a customer base of almost 500,000 users within one year, - owned by Blockbonds AS (listed on Norwegian Stock Exchange)	- aggregates payments for large financial institutions, - provides businesses with alternate payment receipt services, servicing a variety of different consumers, - POS start-up with 100,000 daily transactions (est.)
\multicolumn{2}{c	}{**YELLOW CARD**}
\multicolumn{2}{l	}{- operates through an app which offers cryptocurrency trading services and provides payment remittance services, - more than 10,000 daily users}

Source: Payments Association of Zambia (2023), www.kazang.com, https://yellowcard.io/

Yellow Card's business model is one example of a trend which has diversification from the original classification of traditional financial applications at its heart.

Over the years, the fintech sector in Zambia has attracted several investors. E.g. in 2014, when Mastercard payment card standards were introduced in the country, Mastercard soon began investing in partnerships with local startups such as Union 54. Union 54 was the first Zambian start-up to join the prestigious Californian startup hub Y-Combinator and raised $12 million from international investors.

Public investors also contributed to funding Zambian fintechs. In March 2021 Zambia's Securities and Exchange Commission (SEC) launched a "Regulatory Sandbox", whose guidelines it had developed when partnering with the United Nations Capital Development Fund (UNCDF). The following quote summarizes the intensions underlying the Sandbox:

"A Sandbox is essentially a 'safe playground' in which the testing of capital market innovations can be facilitated under a set of conditions and limitations designed to protect investors ... We believe the Sandbox creates an opportunity for bridging the expectations gap between would-be participants piloting innovations and regulators in an environment that permits a clear understanding of the potential impact on consumers and the financial services ecosystem as a whole"[15]. (www.uncd.org)

---

[15] https://www.uncdf.org/article/6614/zambias-securities-exchange-commission-launches-a-regulatory-sandbox

Lupiya and Premier Credit, both Zambian startups set up in 2019 to operate online lending platforms, were among the first four fintech companies formally selected to explore some digital finance innovation in the Sandbox.

Both Lupiya and Premier Credit started introducing peer-to-peer lending on their platforms at the end of 2021 and launched comprehensive marketing campaigns in the second half of 2022 with adverts being placed along main roads in Lusaka to attract potential investors.

Funding for the advancement of the Zambian mobile payments industry also came from non-government institutions (NGOs) following the introduction of the "National Payment Systems Vision and Strategy (2018-2022)". Financial Sector Development (FSD) Zambia, a UK based fund, spent more than $10 million investing in local projects under the then CEO Betty Wilkinson including funding the establishment of the Payments Association of Zambia (2020).

E-COMMERCE: SHOPPING ONLINE IN BIG CITIES
(by Karin Moder)

E-commerce encompasses both business-to-customer (B2C) and business-to-business (B2B) selling of goods and services on the internet, including the mobile internet sales channel. In this chapter we will mainly focus on the B2C segment and trade in goods. For Zambia, research on e-commerce is still in its infancy, which led us to set up our own survey and gather responses in two consecutive years. The results are presented here and two portraits of e-commerce start-ups enhance the picture.

Compared to other regions of the world e-commerce is still in its infancy in Sub-Saharan Africa. However, a 2021 VISA report emphasizes that growth rates are remarkably high, especially in the leading markets South Africa, Nigeria and Kenya.

"The COVID-19 pandemic has driven customers to eCommerce and digital payment usage: the economic shocks that followed COVID-19 have reduced spending power across the world, including SSA, but the closure of physical stores has provided a growth opportunity for digital payments and eCommerce itself".

In Zambia e-commerce was hardly known before the onset of the COVID-19 pandemic. This is shown by the experience of Tracy Gwendolyn Cheelo - a co-founder of "Find", a Lusaka-based start-up - when she and her Norwegian partner came up with the idea to register a company.

"When we started Find, or in the beginning phases, we had little to no competition, but after Covid hit, we started to see more and more online platforms coming up that offer product delivery in Lusaka".

After longer brainstorming and preparations, the Find pilot website and app were introduced in January 2020. Based on analysis of ensuing market research, www.find.co.zm was officially launched in August 2020. It has since offered a variety of products ranging from body lotions to mineral water and noodles. Until the end of 2020, the Find team had won 200 customers, and took another two years to expand and double the customer base, with break-even expected to materialize in 2023. *"Gaining the trust of the people to buy and pay online before receiving their products"*, is seen as a major challenge by the start-up team. *"That's why quality is key. We try to deliver within 24 hours and we provide 24 hours customer service".*

ONLINE SURVEY RESULTS

Are Zambians ready for e-commerce? What do they buy online and how do they rate their online experience? To gain representative answers to these questions, an online survey was conducted in September 2021 using messenger service WhatsApp, which is widely used among smart phone holders in Zambia. In Q4 of 2022, the survey was updated to accommodate two new aspects and created another 40 responses, which will be presented in detail.

Question no. 1 centres on previous e-commerce experience. Out of the 40 respondents, 80% (32) stated that they had already been shopping online, with 8 of them (20%) indicating having been supported by others in the process. A remaining share of 20% stated that they had no previous experience as to buying online. (Here it is interesting to note that in our 2021 survey the share of respondents with previous online shopping experience amounted to 72.5% and the share of people choosing option "no" had been 27.5%.)

Asked if they would recommend others to buy online, about two thirds of respondents gave a positive answer, about 3% a negative one and about 30% stated that this would depend on the respective seller. This means that about 97% of respondents to this question do not have a negative opinion on shopping online, but see it in either a positive light or have a differentiated stance.

Those individuals with no previous online shopping experience were asked if they intended to do online shopping at some point in the future. It turned out that more than half of them (62%) answered "yes", and that only one respondent gave a clear "no".

When it comes to the most popular goods to be purchased online, consumer electronics and clothing receive the highest score in our survey, with 60% and 50% of respondents making use of these options. Beauty and hygiene products come next with about 27%, food with 10% of entries and finally pharmaceuticals with just one respondent. Besides, there were individual nominations for books, vehicle, art supplies, automotive, jewellery and dog tags. The latter enumeration seems to indicate that the spectrum of goods purchased online could already be rather wide in Zambia and encompasses even specialist product like art supplies.

The frequency of online purchases, however, may not be very high yet compared to other regions of the world. Only 6% of respondents stated to do online shopping several times a week, with most respondents (42%) choosing option "once or twice a year" and 27% option "just once". "Once a month" was provided in 21% of the answers. In two cases an individual comment was given; here "once in a while" and "when need arises" don't seem to indicate high frequency of purchases either.

Figure 7: Frequency of Online Shopping

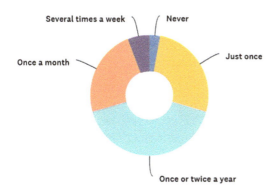

What do we know about the group of respondents? The survey has 22 male (55%) and 18 female respondents (45%). None of the respondents is younger than 19 years and only one person is older than 60 years (2.5%). The highest share of respondents (37.5%), which amounts to more than a third, is found in age group "30-39 years". Age groups "20-29 years" and "40-49 years" are represented with 10/9 respondents (25%/22.5%). Clearly less respondents (5; 12.5%) are attributed to age group "50-59 years".

Figure 8:   Respondents by Age

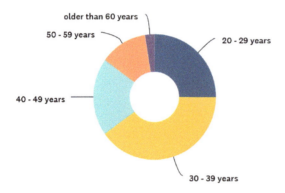

Half of the survey respondents (20) live in the Zambian capital Lusaka, followed by a 32.5% share for Ndola and a 7.5% share for Kitwe. This adds up to a share of 90% of respondents living in big cities with more than 500,000 inhabitants. 4 people (10%) named other residences such as Chibombo, Livingstone (2) and Kasama. All 40 respondents have gone through tertiary education, with 77.5% of them being university graduates and 22.5% college graduates.

In contrast to the 2021 survey, we also received some insights about the specific platforms used for online shopping. It turns out that eBay received the highest share of respondents (53%), followed by Facebook (44%), Alibaba (26%) and Amazon (18%). In two individual comments WhatsApp was mentioned, AliExpress in a different case and "Elgigantan, Bokus, Elendo Eats, Debonairs" by another respondent.

Because of the rather limited number of items which were at our disposal in the 2021 and 2022 surveys we did not include a specific question targeting barriers for e-commerce adoption. We did, however, note the relevant comments provided by some respondents.
- "It is difficult to use a Zambian address to order online through Amazon and other online platforms".
- "Security should be intensified".

It is no surprise that cyber security concerns are raised, and this is in line with user concerns all over the world. The comment about the Zambian address, however, needs to be understood against the backdrop of standardized international e-commerce software, which did in fact sometimes discriminate against users from smaller developing countries or users of domains located in such countries. These cases were known in 2021, but less so in 2022.

Seen in this light, Zambians have profited from the gradual growth of companies offering e-commerce solutions and delivery from Zambia itself. One of the new competitors to early bird online platform "Find" is AfriSupermarket, which started operations in 2021 and had won more than 1,000 customers by January 2023.

Interview with Afshon Wallace Ngige (AWN)
Co-Founder of AfriOnline Group[16]

I: What inspired you to set up an online supermarket?

AWN: I always believed I was probably one of the biggest customers of the service. So it was a no-brainer for me to try and build a product that other people can use. And after starting AfriDelivery and doing deliveries for restaurants, we noticed that our customers always requested for us to pick other things from supermarkets, pharmacies, and other stores that have fast-moving consumer goods. That's how we decided to build a one-stop shop and called it AfriSupermarket.

I: In which year was that?

AWN: AfriSupermarket came after AfriDelivery. We have always had it in mind, but we started the development last year.

I: According to two founders of a different Zambian online shopping platform, the pandemic helped a lot to boost e-commerce in Zambia. Would you agree?

AWN: Yes, I think it was a good catalyst. AfriDelivery was doing pretty well before the pandemic, but the pandemic made it easier for us, when it came to public education, because now people were forced to learn about online shopping and so on. So we didn't have to put too much into marketing. It was very much self-driven. People already knew about it, but they were maybe not curious enough to experiment with it, but the pandemic made it.

---

[16] The interview was conducted on December 15, 2022. AfriOnline Group is the parent company to AfriDelivery, AfriSupermarket as well as AfriWholesale.

I: Where do you operate? Is it just in Lusaka and in the Copperbelt, or do you also operate in smaller places?

AWN: So we just operate in Lusaka, Kitwe and Ndola, that's in Zambia. We are also incorporated in Zimbabwe. That's Harare, we are about to start operations there soon.

I: Would you say that Zambia meanwhile has a strong culture of online shopping?

AWN: It think now it has. When it started, it was a bit shaky, but people here are very curious about technology. A majority of the population, they are very tech savvy. So it has a pretty sizeable market, when it comes to that. There is also very good purchasing power, when it comes to such products. I think, Zambia is a very good market for online shopping, yes.

I: You said there was not so much need for marketing when the pandemic had started. Still I want to ask what's your approach to broaden your customer base?

AWN: We are a very customer-centric business. What I mean is we heavily invest in providing our customers with every good service, with the expectation that they speak about it. We have had very good organic growth where customers are very satisfied with the product and service and then they speak to their friends about it. And we grew like that. Even our traditional marketing – we've not put too many dollars in it.

We also did a lot of third-party strategic partnerships to help us with marketing. So that's in partnership with restaurants or other retailers or distributors. For example, if a restaurant wants to sell food, they can say, ok, we sell food, but if you want to order from us, you have to do it through AfriDelivery.

I: How about the B2B platform? Which goods and services are provided there?

AWN: The B2B platform is called AfriWholesale. That's where we basically do distribution from manufacturers and bigger players to smaller retailers and shops. We recently launched it, a few weeks ago. We managed to get a few distributors and manufacturers under the platform. But the idea here is that we'll be doing distribution for these manufacturers to smaller retailers and smaller shops. So basically you're looking at distributing to smaller supermarkets, shops, restaurants, lodges, hotels – businesses that don't want to sit with too much consignment.

I: What would be typical products?

AWN: We focus mostly on fast moving consumer products. We're talking about sugar, about drinks, about food products basically. Your vegetables and all that stuff. Things that people need to buy mostly on a daily basis.

I: I'm sure you have dreamt really big. So if you can proceed on your road to success, what would be the next big, big success?

AWN: When we formed the group, we tried to build different businesses that could work with each other. In this case we also have another company called AfriStorage. It is a place where SMEs or smaller businesses that sell on our platform can bring their goods. They can list space, based on what they need. So instead of using big space, they can just lease 2 x 2 square metres, both for perishable and non-perishable goods. The idea here is to build an ecosystem that handles storage, distribution and retail. A farmer or business would basically bring their goods to our warehouses, we house the goods, then we load the products on to our platforms. And then we sell on our platforms, websites and apps and now we do distribution for those goods using our assets. That's the motorbikes, trucks and three wheelers.

Our goal is to build that solution perfectly for Zambia and see how we can take it out of Zambia. Currently we're thinking of countries in the neighbouring Southern-African region. Eventually we will see if we can manage to enter a few other countries in Eastern Africa.

I: Who – besides you – owns AfriOline Group? And did the team start together?

AWN: We got four partners. Myself, my German partner, our managing director, who is Zambian, and our Nigerian partner. It started between me and my German partner, more than 10 years ago. Our first business was called AfriTaxi, which was a taxi hailing app in Rwanda. Then we decided to build other products, which we now deploy here. Later on we were joined by our managing director, who works as our active managing director. Her name is Helen. Then the Nigerian partner joined.

I: Do you see increased interest by international investors in African or Zambian tech companies? Has it become easier to attract new capital?

AWN: I mean getting capital has never been easy, especially looking at where we are based. But we see it as a business, so we can bootstrap ourselves until we get to a position where we strategically place ourselves as the next buy-out, in case any of these big partners want to come into the country. We do believe that once we gain some traction on the new businesses, then we have created or formed a full circle that any investor would be more than ready to invest in.

E-EDUCATION: EARLY STEPS AND LATER CHALLENGES
(by Karin Moder)

The COVID-19 pandemic has a reputation for speeding up digital transformation all over the world, including Zambia, and the education sector is no exception. On a policy level, e-education and e-learning were introduced a considerable time ago, just some years after the turn of the millennium. In the following two decades, inadequate funds to purchase ICT devices and develop e-learning platforms and e-content as well as lack of digital skills proved to be the major obstacles to implementation.

The Ministry of Education, through interaction with officers in the Directorate Open and Distance Education (DODE), highlights that e-learning began as pocket initiatives by Non-Governmental Organizations and as sponsored projects in Government learning institutions. With the enactment of the "National Information and Communication Technology Policy" in 2006, gradual progress was witnessed across several government ministries. A National E-learning Committee was established in 2007 and mandated to co-ordinate and promote e-learning. Amongst the achievements was the Government's hosting of the "eLearning Africa Conference 2010" in Lusaka, which drew 1,800 delegates to showcase and share information on e-learning, and planned for uptake of technology for teaching and learning.

The goal of raising awareness for the importance of digital transformation in the education sector was consequently achieved, but implementation turned out to be low because of inadequate funds to purchase ICT devices, develop e-learning platforms and e-content. Partnering with the Commonwealth of Learning[17] and making use of the Open Educational Resources (OER) platform NotesMaster, the Ministry under DODE managed to develop content in 7 subjects for Junior Secondary School in 2017-2019 and upload it on NotesMaster.

Screenshot 5: NotesMaster E-Learning Platform

Source: Video on https://notesmaster.com/ (07/04/23)

NotesMaster, in its Digital Public Goods Library (DPG), provides freely accessible learning materials which can be filtered as to region, subject and grade. The following screenshot shows a selection of subjects, for which e-learning content is available in Zambia as of March 2023. Learning materials consist of files for reading as well as

---

[17] The Commonwealth of Learning is an intergovernmental organization of the Commonwealth, which defines its mandate as providing "access to learning opportunities to those in need, making use of distance education and technologies". (https://www.col.org/about/our-strategy/)

non-locally produced videos with more general content. The local content files were created by Zambian teachers who previously received respective training.

Screenshot 6:   NotesMaster Digital Public Goods Library (DPG)

Source: https://notesmaster.com/library/guest (07/04/23)

Adding to this service, schools, teachers and students are invited to register on NotesMaster and use the platform to conduct live classes online.

After the roll-out campaign in 2019, the advanced option did not yet find many users, which according to the DODE officials in charge at the Ministry of Education, was mostly due to issues of internet connectivity and lack of digital skills training for teachers. After the onset of the Covid-19 pandemic and the closing of schools for longer periods, the Ministry noticed a sharply growing interest in distance and e-learning options, as well as an increased demand for NotesMaster services, with the use being restricted to urban areas, however. By August 2022, a total of 2,500 teachers and 3,000 learners had registered on NotesMaster.

At that time available resources for creation of e-content had not yet been sufficient to cover Senior Secondary School as well. In March 2023 the grades 10-12 gap had been filled by the DODE team with e-content for subjects as Agriculture Science, Mathematics and Civic Education. Training of teachers has been another goal set on the e-learning agenda.

VOCATIONAL TRAINING

When it comes to implementing e-learning, technical and vocational education training institutions are faced with similar constraints and impediments like the ones faced in secondary schools. As Gabriel Konayuma, Senior TEVET[18] Officer at the Ministry of Technology and Science, outlines, "skills are a challenge". His department had few means and opportunities to invest into capacity building before the onset of the pandemic, but due to rather high demand of "emergency remote learning" during the pandemic, additional pathways opened up. In 2021, a total of 28 lecturers coming from 28 learning institutions in all the 10 Zambian provinces received training in online facilitation. The training was facilitated by staff from the Ministry and Technical and Vocational Teachers' College with support

---

[18] TVET is the common abbreviation for "Technical and Vocational Education and Training". The respective learning institutions provide training for school leavers as well as active members of the work force.

from the Commonwealth of Learning. The 28 participants passed on the newly acquired knowledge to others, so that the TEVET department was able to register more than 600 trained lecturers by the end of August 2022. "Leading change for technology", a course in technology-oriented change management, was seen as another capacity building highlight in 2022.

E-learning platforms are still rare to find in the Zambian TEVET landscape with the "Technical and Vocational Teacher's College" (TVTC) being the pioneer with 100% digitization[19]. The college, however, is an affiliate of the University of Zambia (UNZA) and the Copperbelt University (CBU), which might indicate better funding than in standard vocational education institutions, the number of which amounted to 341 as of January 2023[20].

Due to the longer absence of TEVET e-learning platforms, TEVETA (Technical Education, Vocational and Entrepreneurship Training Authority), mostly a regulatory body, embarked on a wide-ranging project to set up a Digital Learning Platform which can be used by all TEVET institutions and their learners. The e-learning platform was finally launched in November 2022 and now provides the first learning materials. On this route TEVETA partnered with the Commonwealth of Learning as well as GIZ, a major German service provider in development cooperation, who funds projects related to water supply and pipe fitting. As Clive Siachiyako, Manager Information, Education & Communications at TEVETA explains, his organization and GIZ are about to create audio-visual content, which will showcase e.g. how learners can start the process of pipe fitting from scratch.

---

[19] http://elearning.tvtc.ac.zm/
[20] https://www.teveta.org.zm/archive/downloads/1674224563.pdf

The long-run goal, however, is to cover the whole syllabus of vocational training courses and to make all courses available as online programmes for learners choosing distance learning. "It's a tedious process. There's a lot of scripting, editing and peer reviewing to be done until the whole process fits the purpose".

Screenshot 7: TEVETA E-Learning Platform

Source: https://www.teveta.org.zm/dlp/course/index.php (07/04/23)

At almost the same time a second Zambia-wide online platform especially for digital skills has been launched in January 2023. TEVETA here partners with the United Nations Capital Development Fund (UNCDF) and IBM who offers free standard courses to Zambians on a dedicated URL (https://sb-auth.skillsbuild.org/signup?ngo-id=0113&mgr=1177815REG). The IBM courses, which are already available and free to use, feature topics such as cyber security analysis, artificial intelligence, cloud computing, enterprise computing and open source software. Tailor-made courses specifically responding to digital skill needs identified in Zambia will be produced in the months to come.

According to TEVETA, production of the new courses on the SkillsBuild platform will be financed by UNCDF as a means to "promote accessible digital economies". The programme targets "entrepreneurs, youths, women and career explorers in the country, particularly in the TEVET sector".

Interview with Dr. Phillip Mwansa
Director of NIPA Distance Learning[21]

I: When did NIPA start providing online courses? Was that during the pandemic or even earlier on?

PM: E-learning was introduced during the pandemic. Previously, we just used to have physical lessons for distance learning, part-time and even full-time. But with the coming of Covid-19, we switched to e-learning teaching and examinations.

I: What were the milestones in setting up the NIPA e-learning platform?

---

[21] The interview was conducted on September 12, 2022 and received an update in 2023. The National Institute of Public Administration (NIPA) is a governmental training, research and consultancy institution. It has campuses for undergraduate studies in three Zambian cities.

PM: One thing we observed was that not all students had access to e-learning platforms. As you may know, Zambia is not so developed in terms of e-learning platforms, so we had problems with students who were away in rural areas. Some students could not manage to buy bundles to be able to access the e-learning platforms, while others had no computers or laptops or even smart phones which could enable them to access e-learning platforms. Those were the major problems which we encountered. So even during examinations, some candidates failed to submit.

I: How could the problems with the devices be solved? Did NIPA have means to lend smart phones or other devices to students? Or did some students have to pause with their courses?

PM: NIPA had and has no capacity to lend devices to learners. The consequence was that students, especially those who were coming for the first time, in first year, dropped or stopped from studies, because they had no laptops and no smart phones thereby affecting our enrolment. Up to now, we haven't recovered. The numbers are lower than they were before Covid-19.

I: Which share of the NIPA courses falls into the category "online courses"? Can you give a rough figure?

All students are expected to do online learning, all units were expected to do online. There is no exclusion. The only one is Law, a course called Moot Court. That's where the division requested for permission to meet the students physically, because there are so many things involved such as assessing somebody's posture. But the rest, whether it is mathematics, IT, Management Studies or business programmes, all of them were conducted through online learning.

I: Did the students who are enrolled and participate in these courses, somehow manage to use ICT devices?

PM: Yes, they did. And those who didn't, had to borrow from colleagues or had to go to internet cafes and pay when they wrote the exam or submitted the assignments. But a good number of them, the majority of them have smart phones. They are able to adapt. Of course, there were others who were not able to and were left behind. There were cases of students who said, "when you are conducting lessons online, we were not following". Sometimes they would be in class, but the internet just drops, or their bundles finish.

I: Are these courses hybrid courses now or are they a 100% online?

PM: Initially, these were in-person training courses, now we just try to transform them or to make them be taught online. As a result, we do not have already packaged online content. In fact, like distance learning, what we have are modules in the materials room, most of them were hard copies. This time we're trying to make soft copies of these hard copies, so that students can just be given the soft copies. But again they complain, some of them are in places where there is no electricity. Others simply don't have gadgets for accessing the materials.

I: To summarize: There's been a lot of progress in creating online courses, but still a lot to do?

PM: Yes, we're making progress and we're insisting now that even when students are attending physical classes, some of the activities like assignments are being delivered using the Moodle platform.

Which means a lecturer prepares learning material and uploads it on the Moodle platform. Then they do their activity and then they send. So what you're referring to as blended learning, could be so. Because we're teaching them physically, but we're giving them assignments using the Moodle platform.

I: If we take a wider perspective, would you say that all higher learning institutions have developed online courses? Is that an established practice?

PM: Yes, a good number of higher institutions have moved towards e-learning. Most of the universities have moved towards e-learning. At the University of Zambia there is what they call "e-campus". Students don't need to go to the University of Zambia, they just register online and start learning.

E-GOVERNMENT: COMPREHENSIVE E-TAX SYSTEMS
(by Karin Moder)

In the final chapter we look at the use of information and communication technologies, particularly the internet, in the public sector. Electronic government (e-government) applies to different kinds of Zambian government institutions. For this topic, we will focus on e-tax systems and learn how ICT companies provide vital interfaces for e-government services. The issue of cyber security will also be considered.

What should we understand by e-government? Britannica uses a definition, which distinguishes between three basic types of e-government interactions.

1. Government-to-government interactions
   Here, technology is used "to enhance the internal efficiency of public bureaucracies, through, for example, the automation of routine tasks and the rapid sharing of information between departments and agencies".

2. Government-to-business interactions
   [They] "typically involve the use of the internet to reduce the costs to government of buying and selling goods and services from firms".

3. Government-to-citizen interactions
   Government institutions use the internet "to provide public services and transactions online and to improve the design and delivery of services by incorporating rapid electronic feedback mechanisms, such as instant polls, web surveys, and e-mail".

One example falling into category no. 3 is e-tax, the ICT based collection and administration of tax revenue, which has seen a rapid development in Zambia in recent years. The Zambia Revenue Authority (ZRA) seeks to increase tax payer compliance and raise tax income, as the lyrics from the ZRA promotional video "Our destiny" imply (https://www.zra.org.zm/about-us).

Zambia, the future is in your hands. The quality of life you desire begins with you. Aspirations and dreams are in your hands. So come and do the right thing. ...
This is our destiny, the future is in your hands. Zambia, do the right thing, this is our destiny.

The direction of the ZRA mission becomes fully transparent through the written call-out *"Pay your taxes for a prosperous Zambia"* at the end of the emotionally charged video.

Provision of e-tax services or digitalization of tax registration, tax returns and payment has been adopted as a major strategy by ZRA several years ago. These developments are clearly in line with steps taken by government institutions in other African countries. This can be seen by looking at the motto of the 2021 International Conference on Tax in Africa hosted by the African Tax Administration Forum (ATAF) in Pretoria: "Domestic Resource Mobilisation: Accelerating Technology for Tax Administrations".

Figure 9: E-tax systems

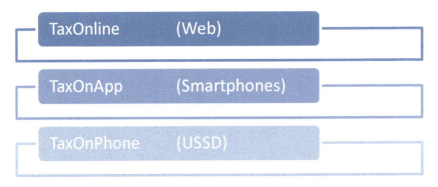

Source: Author's own construction

In Zambia, the phone-based e-tax service, TaxOnPhone, was released in early 2019 through a development partnership with the private sector[22]. The German company ibes AG collaborated with ZRA on this. The idea for TaxOnPhone was developed in a 2018 innovation workshop ("lab of tomorrow") with a number of relevant stakeholders to provide tax services on ordinary cell phones in order to ease compliance and so increase tax revenue from SMEs. The system relies on simple button combinations and does not depend on internet access. "Because of its USSD text-based interface, TaxOnPhone is usable on virtually any cellphone: from the most modest model to the most advanced smartphone", ibesAG describes the innovation[23], pointing out that it can also be used in rural areas where internet connectivity might not be available.

---

[22] Cooperating with ZRA the German Federal Ministry for International Cooperation (BMZ) provided financial support to the project through the develoPPP funding programme, see https://www.developpp.de/en.
[23] https://goodgovernance.africa/ (downloaded on 06/03/23)

As of Q1 2022, around 300,000 Zambian taxpayers have been noted to register on TaxOnPhone. The statistics are shared by ZRA through giz, a German service provider in international cooperation, who supports ZRA to foster good governance and mobilize tax revenue in Zambia. Consultant Cheikh El Wely Sidi Mohamed describes inclusiveness as one of the major achievements of the Zambian e-tax system. "E-services are available for everyone via normal phone, smartphone and PC or laptop. All Zambian business tax payers can reach ZRA services via the three e-tax systems".

In addition to TaxOnPhone, the web-based TaxOnline 2 system for use on PCs and laptops was launched in January 2020.

Screenshot 8: Filing a Tax Return via TaxOnline

Source: https://portal.zra.org.zm/returns/acknowledgeReturn#!

Ten months later, the app-based smartphone version TaxOnApp was introduced[24]. Tax returns can thus be filed both on a computer, a smartphone or a USSD based phone.

As already mentioned, the e-tax modules also provide digital payment options, such as using mobile money or making a transfer through online banking. This involves ZRA partnering with banks and ICT experts creating suitable software for such interfaces. One of these ICT companies is ProBase Group, which is based in Lusaka. The following interview provides further insights into e-governance and e-payments.

Interview with Chinedu Koggu (CK)
CTO of ProBase Group[25]

I: ProBase has been in business for more than 10 years. Inititally, the major goal was to provide professional services in process automation. What customers did you and the other founders have in mind at the time?

CK: Maybe to give a bit of context, the major reason why we opted for process automation was when we saw a lot of software requirements and one of the first cases was our automation business on transaction SMSs. For instance, you go to the bank ATM and use your debit card and your bank sends you an SMS message.

Also whenever you perform a transaction on your account such as if you deposit or withdraw money from your bank account, you also receive an SMS message. That was the initial area we started. But the

---

[24] The IOS version of TaxOnApp was only launched in August 2021.
[25] The interview was conducted on November 19, 2021, and updated on February 15, 2023. Chinedu Koggu moved on to a new employer at the end of April 2023.

main thrust, when we basically established ourselves was, when the Zambia Revenue Authority (ZRA) decided that they wanted banks to create platforms to enable tax clearance. ProBase acquired a customer initiative with Stanbic bank that took a gamble on us to provide tax payment and collection platform that they would then offer to their customers. So that is what I would basically point out as our major entry into process automation.

I: You have already mentioned banks and you have mentioned ZRA. Would you agree that there is always a certain element of PPP in your projects or most of the time?

CK: Yes, it depends on who the end-client is, for instance, when ZRA or any government entity comes up with a requirement, we may most likely work directly with that regulatory entity. However, in the case of ZRA we didn't have a direct relationship with them, instead we had a direct relationship with the financial institutions which ZRA indicated would help them collect taxes on their behalf.

But in other areas we may have a direct relationship with the regulatory entity, for instance, the National Pension Scheme Authority (NAPSA). In the case of NAPSA, we built a platform for the pension body and then also played a secondary role by integrating the pension body's platform to the payment platforms of some of the banks.

So, in that case you note that we played two roles, one role being able to create a platform for the regulatory body and the second one was being able to create a payment platform for the bank clients we have who are also required to extend this capability to their own customers who wanted to pay their pension contributions, taxes or any other services they have.

I: ProBase has built a number of platforms over the years. Judging from your own experience, what does it take to build an accepted and successful platform?

CK: There are two points of view, one being that a client may come and say he/she wants us to build a platform and therefore we have to follow the requirements of the client. And the second is when we seize an opportunity to meet a need that is currently not being fulfilled on the market and then we proceed to build a platform .Therefore we have to be the ones who come up with the business case and sort of interview the clients to get an idea of what they want and then basically produce and push it into the market to see how the product will be received.

There are a lot of requirements from the client. For instance, a client can come to us and say "build for us this platform", but then that does not necessarily translate to what they want, but it translates to what they understand. And when the clients get to use the platform it becomes clear that they actually want something else. So we then also have to facilitate and be able to build the client's specific requirements.

I: What can ProBase do to create a successful platform? What are the practices which determine usage and frequency of usage?

CK: To amplify the question you have just asked, we can make a guess on what we think the clients want and then we can implement our guess or assessment of the market environment. But the adoption or ability of the client to adopt that solution is a totally different problem. For instance, there is a fear for change. So clients will say they are used to this or that and that they do not understand whatever platform we would have designed and brought to them.

Therefore they would not be sure if they would be comfortable using such a platform; so they will be a bit hesitant or reluctant.

However, the government can decide that it wants every company to start paying taxes through such a platform, for instance, starting immediately, next week or next month. In this case, the government will then release new policies or new laws that would drive adoption of that platform. In most cases the government will not leave anyone with any choice in that matter, as it will not be a question of whether you want to pay taxes through that platform or not. So we can then do the best by making the platform easier to use, user-friendly, provide client trainings about the platform and provide trial access over a period of time.

But still the final adoption is typically the standard that the client will have to come to terms with. Therefore the clients also have to make efforts to use the platform or to see if the platform solves their problems. They need to enforce it, too, on their users or staff so as to adapt to or adopt this approach.

I: You also used the term 'user-friendly'. What makes a platform user-friendly?

CK: User-friendly can be anything that affects the ability of the user to easily navigate through the platform without abandoning the process that brought the user to the platform to begin with. For example, when you want to buy airtime, if you find that the process of purchasing airtime is very complicated, the likelihood of completing the transaction or coming back to use that platform again becomes harder.

So the elements required to make it user-friendly will be to make sure that the number of steps required to complete the process are as few as possible .In most cases one should be able to finish the process in two or three steps, nothing more beyond that, because if it gets longer than that then the users can either easily forget what they are supposed to do or how they are supposed to do it.

I: Let's dive more into the ProBase projects ,one of them which went live in 2021 is the Lusaka City Council payment platform .Please provide some information on user-statistics. How many Lusaka residents are able and willing to use this e-government tool and which feature has been mostly used so far?

CK: Confidentiality prevents me from giving explicit details and facts about the LCC payment platform. But there are currently six listed services, and all the said services are operational.

Screenshot 9: Lusaka City Council (LCC) payment platform

https://epay.lcc.gov.zm/home
Browser through the council services that are available to be paid for online

Rates

Ground Rent

Bill Boards Managements

Commercial Rent

Business Levles (Certificates/ Licences/Permits)

Personal Levy

Source: https://epay.lcc.gov.zm/home (presentation in bigger font size)

Three payment methods have been integrated. Firstly, we provide for mobile money payments with MTN, AIRTEL and ZAMTEL, secondly, we offer card based payments and thirdly users can do bank based payments via bank integrations.

We know that adoption of a new platform may take time. So you might spend a year to a year and half to bring the platform to the general knowledge of most people and then to insist that most people who want to make payment should basically utilize the platform instead of coming to Lusaka City Council to make payment manually.

There may still be some elements of publicity and marketing. In 2022, Lusaka City Council thus ran an amnesty campaign to encourage users to take advantage of the platform. The scheme was such that users would pay ONLY 75% of their obligations to LCC, if they utilized the grace period for the amnesty. The programme attracted quite some interest as residents based outsize Zambia made inquiries to facilitate payments. This is one of the benefits or advantages of the platform.

I: I'd now like to focus on human capital and talent in the ICT industry and especially at ProBase group. Where does the company recruit ICT experts and how many employees does the company have?

CK: ProBASE does not recruit any ICT experts. We source talent from the surrounding schools where there is a demonstration of potential, talent, and dedication. This has allowed us to scale to our current size of eighty plus staff with half that number comprising of the development team. We also run an internship program that allows us to assess talent and skill set and thus retain those that meet the criteria.

I: And what's the total number of employees?

CK: We are now sitting at about 80 staff in total with numbers varying based on how many interns we currently are training.

ICT expertise is not only found in the private sector in Zambia, but also in the public sector. Several new departments and institutions have been set up in recent years to facilitate digital transformation. One of them is the Smart Zambia Institute, which is mandated to manage and promote e-government services and processes. This includes enhancing citizens' access to government services and facilitating access to e-government services to improve service delivery as well as coordination of e-government and ICT matters in public bodies. The SZI, a division of the Office of the President of Zambia, draws its mandate from the Electronic Government Act No. 41 of 2021[26]. Electronic services are thus to be provided "in a secure and robust environment".

The latter refers to issues of cyber security, which is a major concern to both public and private internet users. A final interview will shed some light on the scope of these issues and their relevance to Zambia.

---

[26] https://www.szi.gov.zm/?page_id=118

Interview with Misheck Kakonde (MK)
Cyber Security Certificate Holder[27]

I: Cyber security has become a pressing issue in European countries as well as in other regions of the world. Can you outline the general problem for private and public internet users?

MK: Many of us have received friend requests on social media platforms that we were not familiar with. And at times we may confirm the request knowingly or unknowingly. That is the world we live in, where cyber attackers use all forms of schemes to ensure they attack innocent people, who are not cyber conscience or have less information on cyber security.

The list of various schemes for attackers is long. For instance, in Zambia, in many European and most African states scammers and attackers use various sites to attack multiple users such as pornographic link sites. Therefore, all members in each society need to be security conscience and cyber security safe by not opening any weird links from forwarded links as they risk a cyber-attack.

Lene Hansen and Helen Nissenbaum also pointed out as early as 2009 add that threats to cyber security do not only arise from (usually) intentional agents, but also from systemic threats.

I: How are these threats related to Zambia? Can you give some more examples?

MK: Maintaining and updating new technologies is a challenging task especially for young African states, including Zambia. It is

---

[27] The interview was conducted on January 30, 2023. Misheck Kakonde is CEO of Zambian SME Botszam, but lives in Denmark. In June 2022 he received cyber security training at The Hebrew University of Jerusalem.

necessary to protect information and other assets from cyber threats, which may take many forms. The major cyber threat in Zambia, including developed countries, is malware - a form of malicious software in which any file or program can be used to harm a computer user. Different types of malwares include worms, viruses, Trojans, and spyware. Viruses cause dangerous malware in large companies and critical infrastructure such as government information technology departments.

Furthermore, critical departments or infrastructure in Zambia need to look out for ransomware. This is another type of malware that involves an attacker locking the victim's computer system files typically through encryption and demanding a payment to decrypt and unlock them.

Last but not least, Zambia and many African states inhabitants are affected by phishing malware; phishing is a form of social engineering, where users are tricked into breaking security procedures to gain sensitive information that is typically protected. Here, fraudulent email or text messages that resemble those from reputable or known sources are sent. Often these attacks are random and the intent of these messages is to steal sensitive data, such as credit card or login information. A phishing email may be a message such as "you have won yourself a lotto jackpot" or "this is the first lady of Zambia, you have been appointed as our foundation representative, please click this link and pay a sum of k500 to be accepted".

I: How can the business sector cope with cyber attacks?

MK: Business protection against cyber attacks and data breaches is an important aspect in cyber security as it allows for protection of data and networks and thus assured security for end-users. To achieve this, especially Zambian banks need to add features such as improved recovery time after a breach. The recovery time must allow easy phone line systems to the bank or company in times of cyber attack for the company to help its customers from all forms of attacks.

Zambian businesses and especially individual users of social media platforms such as the Meta app or of e-mailing need to ensure they practice prevention of unauthorized user access; this they can be done by always adding the two factor authentication provision.

I: Who is in charge of spearheading cyber security assurance in Zambia?

MK: In Zambia the law that tries to mitigate cyber-attacks is The Cyber Security and Cyber Crimes Bill which was assented into law by the former Zambian President Dr. Edgar C. Lungu in March 2021 and consequently enacted into law by the Cyber Security and Cyber Crimes Act No. 2 (the "Cyber Act") in April 2021.

The Zambia Information and Communications Technology Authority is mandated to develop a safe, secure, and effective environment for the customer, business sector and the government to conduct and use electronic communications. Besides, Zambian citizens and the population at large can advocate for more regulatory compliance.

I: How does the government try to improve cyber security?

MK: Progressive laws on cyber security in Zambia are implemented into law after submissions through the parliamentary select committee on Media and ICT. The committee receives submissions on legislation, policies, and strategies in fighting cybercrimes. Some of the key stakeholders that have so far appeared before our committee include the Law Association of Zambia, the Zambia Police, Drug Enforcement Commission, the MTN part of the network provision companies, the Copperbelt University, Infratel, the Financial Intelligence Centre, the Ministry of Information & Media, the Ministry of Technology & Science, the Ministry of Justice, the Zambia Revenue Authority, the Road Transport & Safety Agency, and other eminent organizations within the cyber security space (National Assembly of Zambia, 2022).

I: What are the prospects for cyber security in Zambia? Are there opportunities coming up as well?

MK: Cyber security is a young industry in Zambia, but with serious boom in line with international standards, especially with the creation of the Ministry of Technology and Science by the United Party for National Development. Zambia happens to be advancing in cyber security readiness through young companies that are on the market, e.g. Sagehill Technologies, Trare Technologies, Botszam Investments and many more.

However, companies and individuals need to be more cyber security conscience and companies need to invest more in cyber security, to ensure prevention of cyber attacks and protection of customers by putting a mechanism for an easy, quicker communication system, when customers are attacked.

OUTLOOK

Our journey through Digital Zambia has come to a tentative ending and we have seen that Zambia has already taken significant steps in terms of digital transformation. In line with Zambia's prevailing poverty and internet connectivity issues the scale of digital transformation may not yet be as high as in other parts of the world. However, the speed of digitization appears to be remarkably high, with the Zambian government acting as a frontrunner in this process. Several government agencies such as the Patents and Companies Registration Agency (PACRA) have already stopped accepting cash payments from their customers in 2023. And when in April 2023, following new legislation, the National Pension Scheme Authority (NAPSA) started offering an option of partial withdrawal of pensions pre-retirement, the claim process was defined and set up as a pure online process.

Besides, the scope of digitalization in Zambia goes way beyond the areas presented in this e-book. E-health certainly is one of the most important fields, where digital transformation has left a greater number of footprints, especially since the onset of the COVID-19 pandemic. E-Farming is yet another example of a sectoral transformation in progress.

Due to low income levels, the cost of connectivity may be a major barrier for inclusive digital transformation and necessitate steps to minimize connectivity costs. However, as much as digitalization may depend on reaching of threshold GDP levels and availability of financial resources, other factors still come in. Interestingly enough, the DQL Index analysts confirm a strong correlation between GDP per capita and the DQL. However, they found a number of countries with lower GDP per capita but better digital quality of life than expected.

"Out of 117 countries, 17 exceeded the expected digital quality of life by providing higher levels of e-security and e-infrastructure, and e-government. They include Ukraine, Armenia, Brazil, Thailand, Serbia, Argentina, Turkey, Bulgaria, Malaysia, Russia, China, Romania, Chile, Uruguay, Croatia, Poland, and Hungary. All three of these pillars have a more significant correlation with the DQL than GDP per capita. This proves the potential to level up the global digital wellbeing with lower resources and more focused strategic planning".
(https://surfshark.com/dql2022/statistics)

The Hichilema government might have found this message inspiring and drawn conclusions which are relevant for planning and policy-making.

Karin Moder

ANNEX:

1. WRITERS' PROFILES

Edna Kabala holds a Bachelor of Arts degree in Economics and Development Studies (University of Zambia) and a Master of Arts degree in Economics (University of Botswana). She also studied Public Management at the University of Illinois under the 2016 Mandela Washington Fellowship Programme for Young African Leaders. Edna is enthusiastic about economic development, financial inclusion and poverty reduction. Currently, she works as a senior lecturer and researcher in the Economics Department of the Copperbelt University. Edna also serves as an Associate Researcher at the Southern African Institute for Policy and Research on a pro-bono basis.

Karin Moder studied Economics at Regensburg, Edinburgh and Frankfurt University and gained professional experience in several fields, including journalism, project management and coaching. She first visited Zambia in 2004-2006 and after returning in 2014 she was drawn to writing about Zambia and providing information about the country both online and offline. After obtaining a Bachelor Degree in Educational Science she intensified project work in Zambia. In 2022, Karin set up a sole trader company, BATCH Solutions, which focuses on holistic adult education through books, arts and travel as well as capital investment in Zambia.

2. WITH GRATITUDE AND JOY

Digitalization is a rather timely topic or a mega-trend – to use a catchy phrase. Who would feel free to say "I have not yet come across it?" Comprehensive data collection, however, has never been an easy mission. It has thus been challenging to do research on digitalization in Zambia and gather sound quantitative and qualitative data. Not all the goals we set at the start could be reached, but we are glad to be able to provide this overview and a base for further research. I'm grateful to all the helping hands and minds on our journey and would like to say a heartfelt thank you.

At an early stage, which was in May 2021, my co-writer Edna Kabala provided crucial inspiration for the future structure of Digital Zambia. Besides, her extensive research on mobile money in the course of her PhD project has been very beneficial for this publication. In a later stage, when Edna's time resources did not allow her to be on the team any more, **Lombe Mufaweli Chibesakundu**, a young analyst, came in to provide some recent information and data.

The chapter on e-commerce has an online survey at its heart, whose design received valuable and repeated input by Günther Boos. I also owe thanks to Dr. Rosa Hettmannsperger for providing guidance before the first survey.

E-education for me was the most challenging topic in terms of research because of lack of statistics and reports. Thus, I am especially grateful to experts such as Inutu Kalumiana, Gabriel Konayuma and Clive Siachiyako who made time to provide information and insights in personal meetings or longer phone calls.

Introductions into e-tax were given to me by representatives of several organizations, including CBU IBIC and giz. I especially would like to thank giz country director Helmut Hauschild for bringing me in touch with Christine Neumann and Cheikh El Wely Sidi Mohamed, the respective experts in his team.

A lot of expertise has also been shared in the full length interviews. I feel gratitude and satisfaction to have these interviews as a vital part in this book. I would also have wished to conduct an interview with a senior representative of the SMART Zambia Institute, but at the time that request could not yet receive a positive reply. A personal meeting in August 2022 with Sydney Tembo, then Principal Communications Officer for Policy Development at the Ministry of Technology and Science, did, however, provide some valuable insights into the goals set for digital transformation by the Zambian government.

The final editing stage has been supported by several people who made time to view parts or even all of the manuscript and give their feedback. I'm especially grateful for the contributions made by Chiyanika Nakasamu, Dr. Bernd Schnatz and Dr. Simasiku Nawa.

Two people stand out in the group of supporters, because they have always been there to listen, discuss and provide ideas and practical support. Rachael Atherton, a dear friend from Edinburgh, managing editor of academic journals for many years, has been one of them. She also is the native speaker who has done the proof-reading for Digital Zambia. Ralf Hillmann, a writer friend, has once again made sure that's the layout of the BATCH Solutions books signals clarity and quality.

Last but not least I would like to thank Prof. Royson Mukwena and Brenda Michelo-Mukata for providing guidance in my efforts to navigate through the necessary steps of getting an ISBN in Zambia, which was a new task for me.

Karin Moder

3. DQL INDEX SUB-CRITERIA LIST

Internet Affordability	- Time to work to afford the cheapest mobile internet - Time to work to afford the cheapest broadband internet
Internet Quality	- Mobile speed - Broadband speed - Mobile internet stability - Broadband internet stability - Mobile speed improvement - Broadband speed improvement
Electronic Infrastructure	- Individuals using the internet - Network readiness
Electronic Security	- Cyber security - Data protection laws
Electronic Government	- Online Service Index - AI readiness

4. REFERENCES

Aron, J. and Muellbauer (2019). The Economics of Mobile Money: Harnessing the Transformative Power of Technology to Benefit the Global Poor.
Available at: https://voxeu.org/article/economics-mobile-money

Adaba, G.B., Ayoung, D.A. and Abbott, P.Y. (2019). Exploring the contribution of mobile money to well-being from a capability perspective. The Electronic Journal of Information Systems in Developing Countries, 1-27.

Bank of Zambia, 2016. "Overview of Financial Inclusion". Presented at the 2nd International Banking and Finance Conference at the Hotel Intercontinental, Lusaka, September 2016.

Chimbulu, B. (2022). Mobile money scammers on the rise, Daily Nation online.
Available at: https://dailynationzambia.com/2022/12/mobile-money-scammers-on-the-rise/

Connecting Africa (2023). Elon Musk's Starlink gets license in Zambia
Available at:
https://www.connectingafrica.com/author.asp?section_id=816&doc_id=785265#close-modalww.napsa.co.zm/the-pre-retirement-lumpsum-benefit-is-here/

de Bruijn, M., Butter I. and Fall, A.S. (2017). "An Ethnographic Study on Mobile Money Attitudes, Perceptions and Usages in Cameroon, Congo DRC, Senegal and Zambia. Final Report".
Available at http://saipar.org/wp-content/uploads/2017/12/ Final-Report-Ethnographic-Study-on-Mobile-Money_March-2017.pdf

Chikumbi L. C. and Siame, C. (2018). "Mobile Money for Increased Financial Access? – We've got Your Back!"

Blog Post. Available at: http://www.fsdzambia.org/mobilemoney-for-increased-financial-access-weve-got-your-back/

Donovan (2012). "Mobile Money for Financial Inclusion". World Bank Publications, 61-73.
Available at: https://doi.org/10.1596/9780821389911_ch04

Kabala, Edna; Mapoma, Rosemary; Nalutongwe, Chitimba; Muyani, Diana; and Lungu, John (2021) "An Ethnological Analysis of the Influence of Mobile Money on Financial Inclusion: The Case of Urban Zambia", Zambia Social Science Journal: Vol. 7: No. 1, Article 4.
Available at: https://scholarship.law.cornell.edu/zssj/vol7/iss1/4

Lusaka Times (2021)
https://www.lusakatimes.com/2021/12/17/government-to-create-an-enabling-legal-framework-that-responds-to-start-ups-and-innovators/

Malakata, M. (2017). Zamtel launches Kwacha mobile money platform. ICT Blog.
Available at: https://itweb.africa/content/Pero37ZxkLDqQb6m

Malakata, M. (2020). MTN Zambia notches up 4.5m mobile money customers. ICT Blog.
Available at: https://itweb.africa/content/mQwkoq6PLQb73r9A

National Pension Scheme Authority (2023). The Pre-Retirement Lumpsum Benefit is Here
Available at: https://www.napsa.co.zm/the-pre-retirement-lumpsum-benefit-is-here/

Ngambi (2016). "Commoditizing Financial Services." Paper presented to the 2nd International Banking and Finance Conference at Hotel Intercontinental, Lusaka, September 2016

Payments Association of Zambia (2022). Quarterly Review. Vol. 2

Pesa, I. (2018). "The Developmental Potential of Frugal Innovation among Mobile Money Agents in Kitwe, Zambia", *The European Journal of Development Research* Vol. 30, 1, 49–65.

President Hichilema, H. (2021): Speech by his Excellency, President Hakainde Hichilema during the Ceremonial Opening of the 1st Session of the 13th National Assembly
Available at:
https://www.parliament.gov.zm/sites/default/files/images/publication_docs/SPEECH%20BY%20HIS%20EXCELLENCY.pdf

Prinslo, L. (2021): "MTN Values Mobile-Money Arm at $5 Billion, Considers IPO".
Available at: https://www.bloomberg.com/news/articles/2021-04-12/mtn-group-values-mobile-money-arm-at-5-billion-considers-ipo#xj4y7vzkg?leadSource=uverify%20wall

Republic of Zambia. Ministry of Technology and Science; UN Capital Development Fund (2022):
ZAMBIA Inclusive Digital Economy Status Report 2022

Rest of World (2022)
Available at: https://restofworld.org/2022/tech-leaders-are-pushing-to-transform-zambia-into-africas-low-tax-startup-hub/

United Nations Capital Development Fund (UNCDF), 2017. The State of the Digital Financial Services (DFS) Industry in Zambia. Blog Article.
Available at: https://www.uncdf.org/map/article/2541/the-state-of-the-digital-financial-services-dfs-industry-in-zambia

UNCTAD (2021): COVID-19 and E-Commerce. A Global Review
Available at: https://unctad.org/publication/covid-19-and-e-commerce-global-review

Welthungerhilfe, Concern wordwide (2022). Global Hunger Index. Food Systems Transformation and Local Governance
Available at: https://www.globalhungerindex.org/pdf/en/2022.pdf

Wikipedia. ChatGPT
Available at: https://de.wikipedia.org/wiki/ChatGPT

Zambia Information and Communications Technology Authority (ZICTA), 2020. ICT Statistics Portal and Database.
Available at: https://www.zicta.zm/

Zambia Information and Communications Technology Authority (ZICTA), 2022. ICTs Sector 2022 Annual Market Report. A Supply Side Assessment of Developments in the Information and Communications Technology Sector

RELEVANT PUBLIC WEBSITES

Bank of Zambia
https://boz.zm/

Inclusive Digital Economy Scorecard
https://ides.uncdf.org/

Lusaka City Council
https://www.lcc.gov.zm/

Ministry of Technology and Science
https://www.mots.gov.zm/

NotesMaster
https://notesmaster.com/

SMART Zambia Institute
https://www.szi.gov.zm/

TEVETA
https://www.teveta.org.zm

Zambia Information and Communications Technology Authority (ZICTA)
https://www.zicta.zm/

Zambia Revenue Authority
http://www.zra.org.zm/

Milton Keynes UK
Ingram Content Group UK Ltd.
UKHW020031211023
430984UK00010B/61